A Thousand Paths to Success

A Thousand Paths to
success

Robert Allen

MQP

Contents

Introduction

We all want success. Our whole society is built on the idea. In former times mere survival was enough of a challenge for the majority of people but now we expect much more. People are engaged in a quest to obtain success both for themselves and their families. But what is success? For many it is all about wealth, possessions, status, and power. They believe that these are the things that make life worth living and they can never be truly happy without them.

This book was not written for such people. That sort of success is shallow and pointless. It offers a mirage of happiness but delivers only misery and dissatisfaction. True success lies in our ability to find a rich, meaningful, and fulfilling life. The successful people in this world have been those who were more interested in helping others than in helping themselves and who showed by their example that we can all be successful if we share whatever happiness we are fortunate enough to enjoy. If that idea appeals to you, read on.

Most Important of All

In order to succeed you must first try. This should be obvious but too many people try to succeed just by imagining it.

Success is whatever you think it is. No one else's definition is worth anything. Only you can decide whether you succeeded.

It is important to think long and hard about what you want out of life. You can have almost anything that you set your heart on but you can never have everything. Your initial choice is the most important you will ever make.

When a man feels throbbing within him the power to do what he undertakes as well as it can possibly be done, this is happiness, this is success.

Orison Swett Marden

Success doesn't come to you. You have to go out and grab it by the ears.

Getting success is a lot more fun than having it. Beware of realizing your dream.

People are attracted to success like iron filings to a magnet. Make sure the people you attract are those who like you whether or not you are a success.

The secret of success in life is for a man to be ready for his opportunity when it comes.

Benjamin Disraeli

Any plan for achieving success only works if you put your heart and soul into it.

Big ideas are fine but a lot of success is about doing the small stuff right.

Don't be afraid to fail. Failure is your best teacher. Every failure is another stone in the foundation of your eventual success.

Success is a temporary state and that's not a bad thing. When you have done it once it's as much fun to do all over again.

Truth, self-control, asceticism, generosity, non-injury, constancy in virtue—these are the means of success, not caste or family.

Mahabharata

When a man is willing and eager, the gods join in.

Aeschylus

What happens to you in life is not that important. What you *do* with what happens is the important part.

Fame and success are different. Decide which you want.

Success can sometimes spring from failure. Don't reject your mistakes, embrace them.

The trouble with success is that you have to keep on doing it. Once is never enough.

Use the bricks people throw at you as the building blocks for your success.

I honestly think it is better to be a failure at something you love than to be a success at something you hate.

George Burns

Boundless enthusiasm,
a *lot* of common sense,
and great persistence
in the face of adversity
are the things that will
see you through.

**Success is getting
what you want.
Happiness is
wanting what
you get.**

Dale Carnegie

To succeed you need
to meet repeated
failure with no loss
of enthusiasm.

You're never
beaten until
you're
willing to
admit it.

Be alert for opportunity. Recognizing it when it comes is one of the most important factors in success.

Try not to become a man of success, but rather try to become a man of value.

Albert Einstein

To laugh often and much;
To win the respect of intelligent people
and the affection of children;
To earn the appreciation of honest critics
and endure the betrayal of false friends;
To appreciate beauty, to find the best
in others;
To leave the world a bit better, whether by
a healthy child, a garden patch or a
redeemed social condition;
To know even one life has breathed easier
because you have lived.
This is to have succeeded.

Bessie Stanley

Success can grow slowly over many years or it can arrive in a moment. The key is to know it when you see it, then grab it and hang on tight.

Genuinely enjoying what life gives you and not yearning for what it doesn't is the secret to success.

Look for the small opportunities that, with care, can be nurtured until they become great achievements.

The thing always happens that you really believe in; and the belief in a thing makes it happen.

Frank Lloyd Wright

What you get in life is the thing you *really* believe in. It is important to think about this carefully—it might not be the thing that you think you believe in.

Success cannot in itself bring you happiness, but happiness is a form of success.

Far better it is to dare
mighty things, to win
glorious triumphs,
even though
checkered by failure,
than to take rank with
those poor spirits
who neither enjoy
much nor suffer
much, because they
live in the gray twilight
that knows not victory
nor defeat.

Theodore Roosevelt

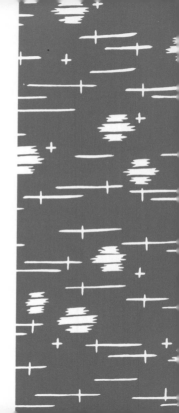

You need not be rich or famous to be successful. In fact, many rich and famous people are failures by most standards.

The truly successful are those who use their good fortune to benefit others.

The way to success is to enjoy every step of the way.

We are all capable of much greater things than we believe possible.

It's not true that nice people finish last. True success only ever belongs to nice people.

Always trying to be the very best you are capable of is the only sure way to succeed.

Success is nothing more than doing the very best you can with what you've got.

There is nothing wrong with failing. We all fail from time to time. What is wrong is when you accept failure instead of letting it inspire you to further efforts and eventual success.

No one can ever defeat you while you refuse to accept defeat. As long as you continue to believe in yourself, you will eventually triumph.

If every day you make up your mind resolutely to do better tomorrow, you will succeed.

Be satisfied with what you have and you will always be wealthy and successful. Be dissatisfied and, even though you may be as rich as a king, you'll feel like a pauper and a failure.

There is no such thing as instant success. Every success that appears to have happened overnight took years of work and struggle.

Life can provide us with almost anything we want. The trick is to know what you *really* want and then go for it with every ounce of determination you can muster.

Success is an opinion. If other people think you are successful that's nice, but you have to consider yourself successful before it really counts.

People will always talk about you, especially when they envy you and the life you lead. Ignore them. You affected their lives, but they don't have to affect yours!

We are what we repeatedly do. Excellence, therefore, is not an act but a habit.

Aristotle

What you can achieve is limited solely by your imagination. If you can dream it, you can do it.

A kite flies high against the wind, not with it.

I would rather be ashes than dust! I would rather that my spark should burn out in a brilliant blaze than it should be stifled by dry rot. I would rather be a superb meteor, every atom of me in magnificent glow, than a sleepy and permanent planet. The proper function of man is to live, not to exist. I shall not waste my days in trying to prolong them. I shall use my time.

Jack London

Keep away from people who try to belittle your ambitions. Small people always do that, but the really great ones make you feel that you, too, can become great.

Mark Twain

Be what you would seem.

Remember to keep going.
Nothing pays off as much
as persistence.

**The only place where success comes
before work is in the dictionary.**

Vidal Sassoon

The common idea that success spoils people by making them vain, egotistic, and self-complacent is erroneous; on the contrary, it makes them, for the most part, humble, tolerant, and kind. Failure makes people cruel and bitter.

W. Somerset Maugham

A successful mind is like a dagger: all the force is concentrated on a single point.

It is easy to avoid criticism: do nothing, say nothing, and be nothing. But if you want to succeed you have to learn to ignore criticism.

Whether you think you can or whether you think you can't, you're right.

Henry Ford

Success that fails to make you and those around you happy is no success at all.

If you think that giving your family money will make you appear successful, you are wrong. What they want is *you* — your love and attention. Nothing else counts.

Whether you are rich or poor, whether your life is long or short, whether you are a king or a cobbler, is all incidental. What matters is that you put every ounce of your being into the things that you do.

Change, develop, and grow.
Success is not possible in
a static life.

**Successful people are wise enough
to improve with age like a good
wine. Only the foolish let
themselves turn sour like old milk.**

Time flies. *Use* your life
and you will succeed.

If I had eight hours to chop down a
tree, I'd spend six sharpening my axe.

Abraham Lincoln

**What you see depends on what you
look for. If you look for success
then, sure as fate, you'll find it.**

Include the success of others in your dreams for your own success.

My imperfections and failures are as much a blessing from God as my successes and my talents, and I lay them both at his feet.

Mahatma Gandhi

Success is not to be pursued; it is to be attracted by the person you become.

Never be afraid that you won't succeed. The only thing to fear is that you never tried.

Every obstacle should be perceived as a stepping-stone to success.

Spend time as you would spend gold. Be determined to make every single day count.

Failure is merely an object lesson in what you should have done to succeed.

Success depends on learning from experience. Let everything that happens to you help build your experience and increase your wisdom. This is the soil from which success will spring.

I think and think for months and years. Ninety-nine times, the conclusion is false. The hundredth time I am right.

Albert Einstein

The most successful men in the end are those whose success is the result of steady accretion…. It is the man who carefully advances step by step, with his mind becoming wider and wider—and progressively better able to grasp any theme or situation—persevering in what he knows to be practical, and concentrating his thought upon it, who is bound to succeed in the greatest degree.

Alexander Graham Bell

Think of the swan that swims with such apparent ease and grace. His success is due to frenzied or furious paddling that goes on underneath.

God gave us two ends: one to sit on and one to think with. Success depends on which one you use; heads you win—tails, you lose.

Run after success and it may elude you but live your life wisely and it will come and find you.

You can be encouraged to succeed but never nagged into it.

Every somebody was once a nobody with a bright idea.

The ladder of success is best climbed by stepping on the rungs of opportunity.

Ayn Rand

Set a goal and achieve it. It doesn't need to be a big goal but, once you learn that you can achieve your dreams, you'll be brave enough to set yourself ever-higher goals.

Ask yourself this question: Whose life has been enriched by my existence? The answer will tell you whether or not you are a success.

Success doesn't always spring from cleverness and big ideas. Plenty of clever people never make it. It has much more to do with getting the little things right.

If you are happy, you are successful. It may not be a success that the rest of the world recognizes but it is real nonetheless.

I long to accomplish great and noble tasks, but it is my chief duty to accomplish humble tasks as though they were great and noble. The world is moved along, not only by the mighty shoves of its heroes, but also by the aggregate of the tiny pushes of each honest worker.

Helen Keller

What people commonly consider success is often nothing more than fame and wealth.

Success is a matter of character. Luck has nothing to do with it.

If you are uninterested in money, fame, or flattery you are in a good position to succeed.

Try to make your success be the cause of success in others.

If things go right, don't let it go to your head. A little modesty looks good on successful people.

Don't trample on others on the way up. Give them a hand as you go. Remember, life isn't a race but a cooperative effort.

Success gets easier as you get older. Once they used to expect me to come on stage, smoke a cigar, and tell jokes. Now if I just get to the stage I get a round of applause.

George Burns

If you can't change the situation and the road to your objective becomes blocked think about changing yourself.

Just as water always flows downhill, power flows to those who know how to handle it.

Always be direct, plain-spoken, and honest. People will then credit you with being subtle, clever, and capable of playing a very cunning game.

We must always change, renew, rejuvenate ourselves; otherwise, we harden.

Johann Wolfgang von Goethe

Success comes to those who learn the lessons of life early. Don't let life flow by you but learn, learn, learn.

Successful people lead by example.

Success is never finished, it is always a work in progress.

Do more for the world than
the world does for you—
that is success.

Henry Ford

**My mother said to me,
"If you become a soldier, you'll
be a general; if you become a
monk, you'll end up as the Pope."
Instead, I became a painter and
wound up as Picasso.**

Pablo Picasso

Only deeds speak.
Words are nothing.

African proverb

People of ordinary ability
sometimes achieve great
success simply because they
don't know when to quit.

Knowledge is power, but enthusiasm pulls the switch.

There is little that is new in the world but success comes from thinking about what is familiar in new and exciting ways.

The penalty of success is to be bored by the people who used to snub you.

Lady Nancy Astor

Don't let success be your access to excess.

If you think you are a success and you act like a success then 90 percent of people will believe you.

To succeed you must cease to regard failure as an option.

**Learn to accept change.
Adaptability is essential in
those who excel.**

Remember that the thin end
of a wedge is a very useful
tool indeed.

**The narrow of vision are
not big of heart.**

Chinese proverb

Men of genius are admired,
men of wealth are envied,
men of power are feared;
but only men of character
are trusted.

Alfred Adler

You are always capable of things you think you can't possibly do.

It is not the critic who counts, not the man who points out how the strong man stumbled, or where the doer of deeds could have done better. The credit belongs to the man who is actually in the arena, whose face is marred by dust and sweat and blood, who strives valiantly, who errs and comes short again and again, who knows the great enthusiasms, the great devotions, and spends himself in a worthy cause, who at best knows achievement and who at the worst if he fails at least fails while daring greatly so that his place shall never be with those cold and timid souls who know neither victory nor defeat.

Theodore Roosevelt

You will achieve far more for the sake of others than you will ever do for yourself.

Happiness and money have this much in common: when you have a certain amount, they both multiply like rabbits.

It is no use saying, "We are doing our best." You have got to succeed in doing what is necessary.

Winston Churchill

In Japan they have little *Daruma* dolls that are weighted at the bottom. No matter how hard you try, you can't knock them over. "Seven times down, eight times up," is a saying every Japanese child knows.

Don't bother just to
be better than your
contemporaries or
predecessors.
Try to be better
than yourself.
William Faulkner

The
Feel-Good
Factor

The best feeling you can have is contentment.

The surest way to feel good yourself is to make others feel good.

If you are going through hell — keep going!

Winston Churchill

The joy you get from life is in direct proportion to your courage.

Happiness and love are there all the time. All you have to do is open your heart to them.

Don't count on being happy in the future. If you can't enjoy the present the future is unlikely to give you what you want.

Tread lightly and live gently.

Money and fame are hard masters. No matter how much you have someone else will have more and you'll wear yourself out trying to catch up.

**Cultivate enthusiasm.
Nothing lights up a life more
than an enthusiastic spirit.**

Set aside a little time for silent
contemplation. You can't feel
good if your whole life is full
of hectic activity.

Throw yourself
wholeheartedly
into whatever you
choose to do.

**No one can make you
unhappy except yourself.**

Success cannot be measured in money but only in the benefit it brings to others.

Success usually comes to those who are too busy to be looking for it.

Henry David Thoreau

Friendship can make you happy even in times of trouble.

Stop thinking, "If only I had such-and-such I'd be happy." You wouldn't. Make up your mind to feel good right now.

Good conversation is always a source of great pleasure.

Laugh loud and often. Laughter lubricates the soul.

Life is a lot like swimming. You can only live it when you have the courage to hold on to nothing and trust that you won't drown.

The ecstasy of religion, the ecstasy of art, and the ecstasy of love are the only things worth thinking about or experiencing.

Don Marquis

We never succeed in making ourselves feel better if we make others feel worse.

It is good to be clever but not at the expense of being kind.

Always be too big
to take offense and
too noble to give it.

**Reckoning up is
friendship's end.**

Irish proverb

When you do good, you feel good. When you do bad, you feel bad. It's that simple.

Live your life one day at a time. It is better taken in small doses.

Never make a habit of being in the right. No one can warm to someone who is always right.

Until he extends his circle of compassion to include all living things, man will not himself find peace.

Albert Schweitzer

**Make room in your life for music.
It lifts the spirits and calms the mind.**

Whatever you do,
don't do it halfway.

Refine your life. Every day
try to make it a bit better.

**A Japanese butcher was asked for
the best piece of meat in the shop.
"It is all the best!" he replied,
"I sell nothing that is not the best."**

There is a joy to
be found in doing
everyday things, well.

Always keep busy. Only those who live energetically are successful.

You don't need to be great to be happy. Small lives well lived are equally as valuable.

People will love
you in spite of
your mistakes
as long as they
believe you always
try your hardest.

Have fun and help others do the same. We do our best when we are having a little fun.

Live your life with the light touch of a surfer. Balance is everything.

People always think they want money but what they really want is fulfillment.

In truth, our children give us endless trouble but we, through the grace of God, regard it as pleasure.

If you do not drive to the woods in sleet, singing, then you have to drive crying.

Czech proverb

An easy
conscience
makes for
a quiet
digestion.

Never grow up completely. There is a child in the best of us who still has hold of the joy of life.

Only the stupid and unimaginative fail to see the mystery of life.

Be as plain-spoken and honest as you can. Success lies in cherishing simplicity.

Timidity is a one-way ticket to misery.

Half the failures of life arise from pulling in your horse as it's about to jump.

Change is natural. All life is change; if you want to be happy, you must learn not to resist but to embrace change like a brother.

If your aim goes astray that is annoying but if you had no aim to begin with that is tragic.

Chop your own wood and you will be warm twice.

Henry Ford

Do as much good as you can, whenever you can. Even small acts of kindness will enrich your life.

What we think we need in life is comfort, but what invigorates us the most is challenge.

Doing
difficult but
necessary
things is
one of
the ways
in which
we grow.

The coward in all of us says, "I can't, I shouldn't," but you can and once you dare you'll be proud of yourself.

Feeling genuinely happy for other's successes can make you feel more positive about yourself.

The more you become attached to things, the more you will suffer. Learning about all of the things you can do without will liberate you.

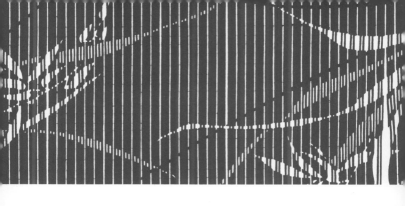

A walk in the countryside, breathing fresh, clean air— there are few things that can make you feel better than that.

The best is the
enemy of the good.
Voltaire

**When you feel bad, get up
and do something. Activity
has the power to take away
all kinds of pain.**

People always talk about "working hard." Work, if it is done with enthusiasm, is pleasant and leaves us feeling satisfied—it doesn't have to be hard.

Stretch yourself in every way—mentally and physically. It is only when you have been fully stretched that you earn the right to relax.

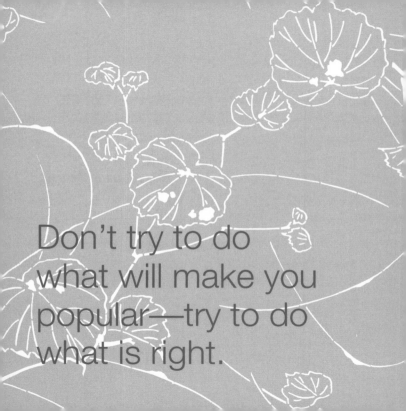

Don't try to do what will make you popular—try to do what is right.

Spend little time trying to find ways to make yourself feel good. Concentrate on doing what you should and you'll find that you feel good enough.

Don't hold on to bad feelings. We are all plagued with negative emotions from time to time but the secret is not to nurture them; instead, we should let them pass from us as soon as we can.

Never plague yourself with regrets and remorse. There is nothing that you can do about the past so don't let it poison the future. Move on and do better next time.

Think of your life as though someone were writing your biography. What would you want them to say about you? Whatever it is, make sure that you provide them with the right material.

To be doing good deeds is
man's most glorious task.

Sophocles

**Noble deeds and hot baths are the
best cures for depression.**

Dodie Smith

To be happy you should
never do what you would
undo if caught.

Occasionally you may have to tell lies to others if only to spare their feelings, but always be honest with yourself.

Anyone who succeeds in life will be surprised to discover how many old friends he has.

Learn to like yourself. This may seem obvious but many people are miserable in life just because they haven't taken the trouble to do this.

Flowers often grow more beautifully on dunghills than in gardens that look beautifully kept.
St. Francis de Dales

You will only be wise and safe if you are honest.

Look people in the eye and tell them what you think. Never smile and say what you think they want to hear.

Today's achievements are so often yesterday's impossibilities.

Joy is what it feels like to grin all over the inside of your face.

Joy arises simply from doing that which is worthwhile, really well.

Joy is not found in things. It can only be found hiding within yourself.

Pleasures come and go, but joy abides.

Your emotions affect every cell in your body. Mind and body, mental and physical, are intertwined.

Thomas Tutko

Laziness always looks attractive but it is a slow, sure poison.

Get rid of routine. Surprises make life worth living.

The length of your life is less important than what you do with the time you have.

To live at all is miracle enough.

Make sure that you live while you live.

Go out and attack life — it's going to kill you anyway!

Whoe'er among his fellows
  wins a name
Soon learns that envy is the
  price of fame.

Arthur Barry O'Neill

**Don't worry too much about what
life is for; get on with living as well
as you know how.**

In between goals is a thing
called life that has to be
lived and enjoyed.

Sid Caesar

**The best things in life—
love, friendship, and loyalty—
are available without charge
to all who want them.**

Life is not like a novel: you have to do the best you can even though the plot makes no sense.

There could be few things in life more miserable than becoming accustomed to luxury.

I never had a policy; I have just tried to do my very best each and every day.

Abraham Lincoln

You express true love by letting people go, not by hugging them to you.

In real love, you want the other person's good. In romantic love, you want the other person.

Margaret Anderson

Look forward to the adventure of tomorrow.

A successful
life isn't
about work,
money,
or ideals—
it is about
people.

Every life has a story and, if we are fortunate, a happy ending.

Grab life by the hand and ask it, "Where do we go next?"

If you're not careful life will happen to you while your back is turned.

Happy the man who never
puts on a face but receives
every visitor with that
countenance he has on.

Ralph Waldo Emerson

When Japanese artist Hokkusai talked of his long life he dismissed as worthless all the work he did before he was 50. It was only when he reached 70 that he felt he was really turning out work of worth and when he lay on his deathbed at 89 he said, "Ah, if only heaven had granted me five more years I would have been a real painter."

**Put all your eggs in
one basket—and
watch that basket!**

Keep within you
the heart of a child.

Live your life as though you were never going to die, but live each day as though you might die tomorrow.

Improve yourself a little bit at a time. Sudden changes never stick.

The journey of your life should never end until the day you die. Keep moving for there is much to do.

Enthusiasm is contagious. Why not start an epidemic?

If God had wanted us to fly, he would have given us wings. And he did.

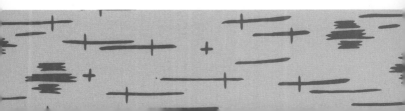

If a man is called to be a street sweeper, he should sweep streets even as Michelangelo painted, or Beethoven composed music, or Shakespeare wrote poetry. He should sweep streets so well that all the hosts of heaven and earth will pause to say, here lived a great street sweeper who did his job well.

Martin Luther King, Jr.

The problem about winning the rat race is that you remain a rat.

Never postpone joy.

Your talent is what you are given by God. How you make use of it is up to you.

If I had but two loaves of bread, I would sell one and buy hyacinths, for they would feed my soul.

Koran

Don't worry about the future. You are building the future right now.

Think for yourself. Letting others do your thinking is like letting them eat your food for you.

The Japanese say, "Speak of tomorrow and the devil laughs." The future is never as we imagine so try not to worry about it.

Don't be a someone—always be a something.

It's too bad I'm not as wonderful a person as people say I am, because the world could use a few people like that.

Alan Alda

Somewhere—where, we do not know—is something truly amazing waiting to be found.

This day will not come again. Inch time—foot gem.

Zen saying

You are nothing but potential bursting to be realized.

Love conquers all.

Virgil

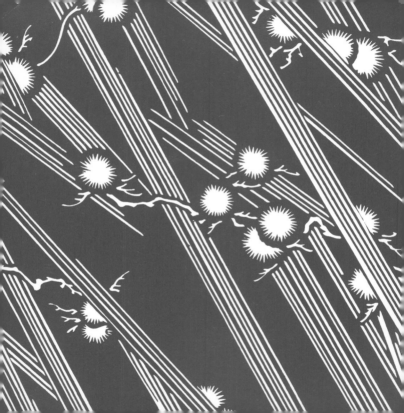

Things of
the Spirit

Spiritual progress and worldly success are not compatible. You have to make a choice.

Simplify, simplify, simplify! A hectic, complicated life leaves you no room to succeed in higher things.

People think that you need to be tough to succeed in worldly matters. But to succeed in matters of the spirit is what takes real strength.

Your progress should always make others happier. Nothing that causes pain to those around you can ever lead to spiritual satisfaction.

Always keep going. The road is long and hard but you must keep traveling even when you think you can't continue.

Always keep a sense of humor and a sense of proportion. Never lose sight of these.

Look for the good in people. What is bad is usually ignorance and fear.

No amount of worldly success will ever compensate for the lack of a quiet, contented mind.

Always ask, "Why?" and never be satisfied with the answer.

Never be happy with yourself as you are. Constant improvement is the only thing that will help you grow.

Don't cling to the things you have done. Throw them away and do something new and better.

Always be open to new ideas. Only the stupid and the dead fail to change.

If you think you know the truth you are deluded. Only those who know that they do not know are wise.

Humans have a habit of achieving anything they set their minds to, good or bad. Be sure that you work only for the good.

"Birds of a feather flock together," according to the proverb. Associate with good people and you will find that you become good.

Everything changes; nothing remains the same. If we resist change we suffer. The wise learn to embrace change.

Why do you always seek the answer? You already *know* the answer.

The fire of enthusiasm drives you on, but a fire in the hearth makes you drowsy.

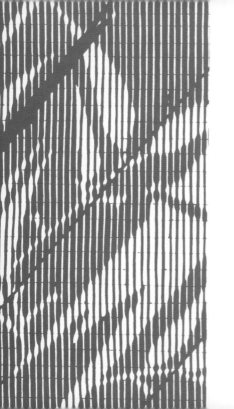

Strength of purpose is the stick that helps you climb the stoniest path.

However fine your words, you will be judged by your actions.

The world is full of teachers whose knowledge will help you. All you have to do is look for them.

Don't speak unless you have something to say. Always listen.

You will never succeed if you follow others. We each have our own path and must cut through the jungle on our own.

Don't look for approval from others but have a sure sense of what is right for you.

Your mind is a garden. Pick out the weeds and plant flowers in their place.

Stay calm in the face of trouble. A cool head will solve problems but a hot one will create more.

There are things you can change and things you can not. Learn to know the difference.

When others lean on you it is they who are holding you up.

What you do to benefit others benefits you far more than what you do to benefit yourself.

All life's troubles
help to educate
a receptive mind.

Life is full of alarms and distractions. Keeping your mind focused is a skill we need to cultivate.

Live in the present and let the future take care of itself. The future is never what you think it will be.

Don't waste time. It will never come again and you need all you can get.

Success in matters of the spirit can often look like failure in matters of the world. Which is more important to you?

Be in charge of your own life. It is too important to leave to others.

Be courageous.
Even the quietest life
tests our courage to
the limit.

Whatever you do, life goes on. But you can help to make it better or worse.

Burn yourself up in your activity. Like a good fire, your life should consume you completely.

Modern people are impatient. They want fast food, fast cars, and instant gratification. But the road to spiritual knowledge is long and slow. There are no shortcuts.

Be a good friend to those around you. Always consider your duty to them before thinking of your own convenience.

The things you desire are dangerous (especially if you get them).

Courage is not about having no fear. It is about being fearful but still doing what you must.

The truth is what we all strive to find. But it is rarely plain and never simple.

Always be honest with yourself.

Always aim to surprise yourself with the heights to which you can climb.

Don't waste time judging others. There is plenty of room for improvement in yourself.

Always be
prepared to
do for others
more than
they would be
prepared to
do for you.

This life is not
a practice.
Everything you do
is the real thing.

There is no one part of your life that is labeled "spiritual,"—the whole of your life is a spiritual matter.

Is benevolence really far away? No sooner do I desire it than it is here.

Confucius

Never look down on anyone unless you're helping him up.

Jesse Jackson

Struggle to free yourself from attachments as a prisoner struggles to free himself from chains.

The emperor said, "I have built temples, paid for monks and nuns to be ordained, given charity to the poor, and employed many scholars to produce copies of the sacred scriptures. What now is my merit?" To which the sage answered, "None at all."

Strive to live in the present. The past and future will lead you astray.

Pay attention to children. Just as you help them, they can also help you.

Keep promises.
Make sure people know
they can trust your word.

**Strive to be yourself, and strive
to know what that means.**

The world's most
powerful word
is "why."

Don't let success in the world spoil you. Always keep the virtues you had before you succeeded.

Never be satisfied with
your progress. Spiritual
development never ends.

**Try to stay calm no matter
what life throws at you.**

Don't worry about death.
You won't be there when
it happens.

Don't be moody or irritable with those you love.

Keep stillness at the center of your being.

Make your paradise the place where you are right now.

Take your happiness
wherever you find it.

**Be satisfied with what
life gives you. Constantly
striving for more will
aggravate your spirit.**

Don't be so caught up in your own journey that you neglect to help others on theirs.

Life is a team game. We have to learn to play together.

Always expect that things will turn out fine, but have an alternate plan ready in case they don't.

Before you speak, pause to consider your reaction if someone said those words to you.

Taking the first step is always the hardest. Make up your mind and set off resolutely.

Hate can look frightening but love is eventually stronger.

Never bear grudges. They do you more harm than anyone else.

Guilty secrets have a strange habit of leaking out. Better to get rid of them before that happens.

Whenever someone says something that upsets you, imagine that he or she is a friend of yours. How would you react then?

Do not constantly compare yourself to others. That path only leads to discontent.

Always try to keep a cheerful face and happy disposition. It will make you and all those around you feel better.

Seek out people who you can admire and emulate.

Be blind to the faults of others and unaware of your own good points.

Life is a mountain that we climb day by day. The climb is easier if you keep company with good people who help each other.

Hold your achievements lightly. There are few sadder sights than an old person bragging about what he or she achieved long ago.

Don't sing your own praises. That is work for others to do. Your job is to give them plenty of material to work with.

Stay close to nature. That is where you see real success at work.

Be eager to travel in your mind. Always seek out that which is new.

Listen to others even if what they say initially sounds odd. Don't be in a hurry to tell them they are wrong.

Trust in the power of the good. It will always repay the confidence you place in it.

You influence others
even when you are
unaware of it. Make
sure that the influence
is always a good one.

Tell the truth but do not use it
as a weapon to wound others.

Be a peacemaker in small matters as well as large ones. Be the cause of peace in others.

Remember, your world is nothing but mind. The state of that mind is up to you.

Remember that you are living in what you will one day call "the good old days."

Always keep busy. Idleness is a destructive thing.

Be generous in all things. The more you give to others the more you receive.

When there are breaches with others, make sure that you are the one who is first and most persistent at trying to heal them.

Thoughts quickly become actions, so make sure all your thoughts are good ones.

Evil actions done in the name of religion are doubly damned. Make sure your religion only calls for you to do good for those you meet.

You will be
precisely as
miserable as
you think
you are.

A rigid mind is a symptom of a cold heart.

Honor and disgrace are things that startle. What does this mean? Honor startles others when it is conferred and when it is taken away.

Tao Te Ching

Anybody will do things for money. Try to be better and do good for no money.

Build character as termites
build their mound—little by
little but eventually very high.

**Be a well. People draw
from a well constantly but
the supply never runs out.**

Be the one people know they
can rely on in times of trouble.

**For the body—water;
for the mind—purpose.**

Work to be
the master
of your fate.

**One day someone will write
your eulogy. Make sure you
give them plenty to say.**

Leave the world in better shape than when you found it.

Whatever you do, pause afterward to consider how it could have been done better. Improvements can always be made.

The only life worth living is one you have made that way.

Humanity's journey is always uphill. People were made to climb.

If you love people you accept them just as they are. Wanting to change people to suit ourselves is the root of half the trouble in the world.

The power of good is strong in the world. Don't let anyone tell you different.

No matter what you have done, there is always a chance to stop and do better.

As you grow older your true personality emerges. Look inside yourself and decide how you want people to see you once youth has left you.

Try not to give advice; instead teach by example.

We all reap what we sow. Buy only the best seed.

Humans have an uncanny knack of being able to do whatever they set their hearts on. Therefore set yours only on things that are good.

Never use God as an excuse to do things that God would despise.

Let each day be a new dawn bright with hope for the future.

The world is a strange and mysterious place. Study it carefully and never take it at face value.

Laugh a lot and be the cause of laughter in others.

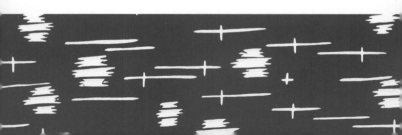

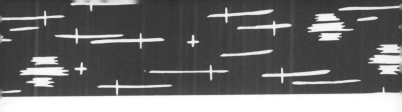

Always be
prepared to say
you are sorry.

**You have within you the
seeds of greatness. All
you need now is the water.**

In the end it comes down to this: Do you believe that we are apes clinging to a piece of rock or does life inspire you with a feeling of mystery and veneration?

Things of
the Mind

It is important to realize that there is no outside to the mind.

Thoughts lead to words and to actions. The wise control their thoughts carefully.

You wouldn't fill your house with garbage. Treat your mind with the same care.

The mind is the most capricious of insects—flitting, fluttering.

Virginia Woolf

It is as important to keep the mind flexible as it is to exercise the muscles and sinews of the body. A rigid mind is a terrible affliction both to its owner and to others.

Decide by all means, but bear in mind the possibility that you are mistaken.

Your whole world is nothing but mind and you will never know anything except mind. Is it not worth paying it careful attention?

The unexamined life is not worth living.

Socrates

Curiosity is
the means
by which
we humans
constantly
develop
the mind.

Having a good mind is one thing—learning to use it well is another.

Education should encourage the mind to expand, not just furnish it with knowledge.

Learn to trust that part of the mind that you can't see.

Language, however imperfectly, helps minds grow together.

The human mind may march forward slowly but it never stops.

One sees the mind is always demanding to be certain, to be secure, to be safe. A mind that is safe, secure, is a bourgeois mind, a shoddy mind. Yet that is what all of us want: to be completely safe.

Jiddu Krishnamurti

If you do not take the trouble to control your mind, it will certainly control you.

A mind that is made up too easily will never grow.

Memory is said to be the library of the mind. But be careful—it doesn't always produce the book you were looking for.

Only a fool blurts out
everything that is on his mind.

A peaceful mind is
a powerful mind.

All problems exist only in the
mind and it is within the power
of the mind to resolve them.

Knowledge is the fuel of the mind.

Superstition is
a disease of
weak minds.

A great mind thinks nothing but generous thoughts.

Memory is not a clever trick for finding your car keys—it is who and what you are.

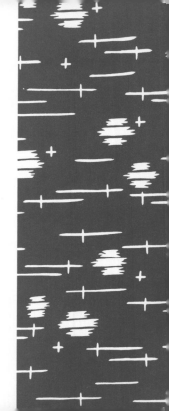

Nothing in life is as good as
the marriage of true minds
between man and woman.
As good? It is life itself.

Pearl Buck

**Our minds are like crows.
They pick up everything
that glitters, no matter how
uncomfortable our nets get
with all that metal in them.**

Thomas Merton

Little minds are fit
only to shrink.

Every work of art represents
an exploration of the mind.

Physical activity
helps to promote
an active mind.

All our fears are but a disease of the mind.

An idle mind is the devil's workshop.

Proverb

Wine frequently reveals the true state of our mind.

The strength of the body is limited but the strength of the mind is not.

It is often hard to make the mind face trouble squarely.

A butterfly mind is of use only to butterflies.

The world of mind is a comfortable Wombland, a place to which we flee from the bewildering queerness and multiplicity of the actual world.

Aldous Huxley

Teachers used to say, "An untidy desk shows an untidy mind." The tidy-minded are the curse of this world.

A good walk brightens a sluggish mind.

Mind is like a muscle—if you want it to stay in good shape you have to use it regularly.

Courage may involve the whole body but it starts with the mind.

A mature mind knows that there are no neat answers.

The mind is like a pond. If you keep agitating it, the mud will cloud it completely. Let it settle, let the water clear by itself.

The best mind-altering drug is truth.

Lily Tomlin

Be a master of mind
rather than mastered
by mind.

Zen saying

Your thoughts are who you are. Be careful what you let yourself think.

The mind is a tricky, devious thing. Grasping it is like trying to catch a fish in your hands.

Mind over matter is simply a false distinction.

Left to itself the mind often wanders down interesting paths.

Everything you can imagine is real.
Pablo Picasso

Almighty God influences us and works in us, through our minds, not without them or in spite of them.
Cardinal Newman

A strong mind makes for a healthy body.

Every day make the effort to improve your understanding.

A strong mind harbors only kind and generous thoughts.

For some the life of the mind is an alternative to the life of the body. To the wise, they are one and the same.

Always try to imagine the world as others see it. A change of perspective can be very beneficial.

Fill your mind with all the learning and experience you can get hold of. It is always hungry for material to work on.

We take the mind too much for granted. As long as everything appears to work normally we ignore it. Try doing that to your car and see how far you get.

Exercise for the body is medicine for the mind.

Hardly anybody, except perhaps the Greeks at their best, has realized the sweetness and glory of being a rational animal.

George Santayana

Never hesitate to think the unthinkable. That is how progress is made. Suppose no one had ever dared to question that the Earth is flat?

Like a good knife, the mind grows sharper if it is kept in constant use.

If you have a quick, clever mind you are fortunate. If you despise those who are less quick and clever then you do yourself harm.

Keep your thoughts positive and cheerful. A gloomy mind is not an asset.

Do not accept any limit to your potential. The human mind is the most remarkable and complex construction we know. We have hardly begun to understand all that it can do.

Bright minds cast their light on one another.

A quiet mind need not be an inactive one. Chewing on a good problem keeps your wits sharp and your mind relaxed.

As with the body, in order to remain supple your mind needs to bend and stretch in as many ways as possible.

Do not let your mind entertain bad thoughts. Remember how one bad apple can rot all the others in a bushel.

Music not only soothes and relaxes the mind but also provides food for thought.

I am incurably convinced that the object of opening the mind, as of opening the mouth, is to shut it again on something solid.

G. K. Chesterton

Meditation is both exercise and nourishment for the mind. It will repay the time you invest in it many times over.

Many things are damaging to the mind—drugs, alcohol, gambling, lust, hatred, envy—the list is a long one. Avoid all these things if you would live well.

Minds affect one another. Only let yours associate with people whose influence will benefit you.

Everyone is attracted to a kind and generous mind.

The human mind is endlessly curious. This is one of our greatest strengths. Go and find out! It doesn't matter what you find as long as you never give up searching.

The mind is constantly inventing but, to do its best work, it needs some encouragement. Challenge yourself constantly to come up with ideas that are new and interesting.

When
you give
someone a
piece of your
mind it is
always the
wrong piece.

The most interesting parts
of the mind are hidden.
But they will speak to you
if you keep quiet long
enough to let them.

**Few of us make the most of our
minds. The body ceases to grow in
a few years; but the mind, if we will
let it, may grow almost as long as
life lasts.**

Sir John Lubbock

Once you have made up your mind about what you really want to do all the rest is a matter of detail.

The real training of the mind is not done at school. It is accomplished by a lifetime of intellectual curiosity.

The little word "why" is a powerful tool for an inquiring mind.

A guilty mind is never free even though the body remains at liberty.

Power is attractive only to undeveloped minds.

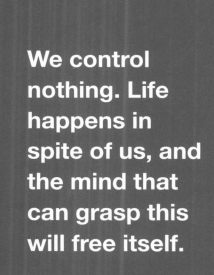

We control nothing. Life happens in spite of us, and the mind that can grasp this will free itself.

Be ruthless in throwing out thoughts that are unworthy of you.

Of all the things I've lost, I miss my mind the most.

Mark Twain

Every great discovery, every revolution in thought, started life as a passing notion in someone's mind.

Look at life honestly and you will see that nothing is tangible. In time everything passes from us. Accept this and get on with your life.

Everyone who has the ability to think well possesses a mighty empire.

The discovery that the mind can regulate its thoughts, fostering some and dismissing others, is one of the most important stages in the art of self-culture. It is astonishing how little this art is practiced among Westerners.

John Cowper Powys

A creative mind has no more chance of being tidy than a busy workshop.

Try to work on several projects at once. It is an amazing quality of the mind that thinking about one task will inspire helpful thoughts about others.

A strong mind and a hard heart never go together.

Even the wisest
minds are only at the
beginning of all there
is to learn.

A foolish consistency is the hobgoblin of little minds.

Ralph Waldo Emerson

Anger blinds the mind.

An enthusiastic mind will lighten the heaviest burden.

A closed mind repels people as surely as a locked door.

Success or failures lie entirely within the mind.

No mind,
however loving,
could bear to
see plainly into
all the recesses
of another mind.

Arnold Bennett

The only real magic
is the powerful magic
of the mind.

**Think always, who is
the thinker that does
the thinking?**

Minds that work together may be stronger than those that work alone.

Have you ever noticed how hard it is to express exactly what is on your mind? All art springs from this.

Religion is the attempt of the mind to find its source.

Happiness dwells nowhere but in the mind.

Never forget to lighten your mind with regular doses of laughter.

Minds do not wear out with constant use but, if left unattended, they can rust.

A mind made up
should not signify
all thinking finished.

Friendship is
one mind in
two bodies.

Mencius

Imagination is the magic carpet of the mind.

Lack of humor is a disease of shallow minds.

Pain of the mind is worse than pain of the body.

Age is an issue of mind over matter. If you don't mind, it doesn't matter.

Mark Twain

Only a weak mind seeks ultimate answers. There is no ultimate knowledge, only the endless challenge of discovery.

When your body wants to give up your mind says, "No, keep going!"

A mature mind does not crave certainty.

It would be better to have an ugly face than an ugly mind.

Look at your mind. Watch the thoughts rise and fall. See how they come and go and never stay in one place for long. What creature is this with such a fluttering candle flame for a mind?

The mind can also be an erogenous zone.

Raquel Welch

The mind produces all that is best and worst in us. It produces endlessly without compunction. It is up to us to refine what comes out of this cornucopia of thoughts.

The narrowness of the mind is usually matched only by the width of the mouth.

Things of
the Body

You paint your house, freeze your food, and have your car serviced. The body is no different—if you want it to work, it needs to be maintained.

Laugh heartily and often. There is nothing that lifts the spirits as much as a good laugh.

Treat your body kindly and listen to what it tells you. Don't force it to do things that injure it.

Do not be overly proud of your body. Beauty and strength are fleeting things. Enjoy them while you have them but be prepared to let them go.

A healthy body will make for a quiet and contented mind.

Do not be led astray by the senses. Like children, they are easily excited by trivial things.

Get plenty of exercise. Your body will repay the effort many times over.

Do not worry about the passing years. A healthy body will last you long enough.

Your body is in your mind; your mind is in your body. The world is mysterious and hard to understand.

Always watch the world carefully. Try to see what is really happening. Nothing is the way it first appears.

The best way to avoid illness is to take care of your body before it gets sick.

Your body always knows what is best for you—remember to listen to it carefully and it won't let you down.

We have so many words for the states of the mind and so few for the states of the body.

Jeanne Moreau

We aim to control the mind but we must start with control of the body.

Movement used wisely has a wonderful power to improve our physical, mental, and emotional life.

Always dance—for dancing lifts the spirits and enables the mind.

Modern life increasingly takes things out of our hands and gets machines to do them instead. The machines get no benefit from this but we lose something important to us.

Keep active at all times. It is important to have slightly more to do than you can actually manage.

Our hands are not only for grasping.
They are good for giving too.

**If you would not lose your mind,
remember to look after your body.**

All of us over 40 have the face
we deserve.

**The body is a source of great
trouble. When I no longer have a
body, what trouble have I?**

Tao Te Ching

Remember, the body has one inviolable rule: use it or lose it.

Grace is to the body what clear thinking is to the mind.

La Rochefoucauld

If you punish your body it will always return the favor with interest.

People say, "The spirit is willing but the flesh is weak." Not so. The flesh is strong.

Always walk as tall as you can. If you walk tall you'll feel good and behave well. Don't trust slouchers.

Bless your body always. Speak no word of condemnation about it.

Rebecca Beard

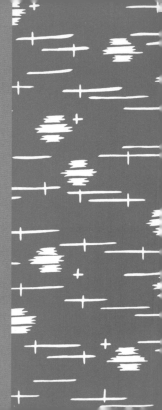

The physical is not second best to the spiritual; the two are different aspects of the same thing.

Think with the whole of yourself— body and mind working together.

Hands have as much wisdom as heads. Who plays a piano with his head?

People say athletes have their brains in their feet. It's better than having no brains at all.

Love has the power to warm even the coldest of us.

Don't be so clever that you use technology to save you the trouble of grasping the world in your hands.

We long to touch. We ache with a curiosity to feel. Yet often we are too embarrassed. What a missed opportunity!

Feel life with every muscle and every nerve. Unless you put your whole body into it, you'll never understand what life is all about.

The body is a big sagacity, a plurality with one sense, a war and a peace, a flock and a shepherd.

Friedrich Nietzsche

How extraordinary that we let bad hair ruin a whole day.

Don't worry about those wrinkles. They are the evidence that you have truly lived.

The body depends on the world for its sustenance. Why then are we so eager to harm the very thing that feeds, clothes, and shelters us?

You are what you eat. Everybody knows it but very few do anything about it.

Bodies are delicate. The wonder is not that they get damaged but that they survive so long.

Your body is where you live. Would you neglect to repair your house? Then make sure you look after your body as it deserves.

Fine art is that in which the hand, the head, and the heart of man go together.

John Ruskin

There is something about bodies that makes them want to compete with each other and decide which is the fastest, the strongest, the most graceful. In this way we climb to ever greater heights.

Dance expresses the entire range of human emotions.

The body has wants and needs. Supply the needs but restrain the wants.

Think of the body as a hostel where you live, for now.

Pain is an opinion.

Watch other people carefully. Bodies often speak much louder than words.

Why are some religious people so disturbed by the body? Do they think we can do without it?

I hope you are more comfy and freer from pain. Sometimes I think the resurrection of the body, unless much improved in construction, a mistake!

Evelyn Underhill

Move gently and before you move, look.

**Beautify your body if you wish.
But remember what is going to
happen to it eventually and don't
become preoccupied with vanity.**

Give someone a helping hand
whenever you can.

**They say that the eyes are
windows to the soul. What
can people see of your soul?**

The best and most beautiful things in the world cannot be seen or even touched. They must be felt with the heart.

Helen Keller

Moderation is the best medicine for your body.

If you feel you don't have time to relax that is when you should do it.

Remember that old age is always 15 years older than you are right now.

**The pressure of the hands causes
the springs of life to flow.**

Tokujiro Namikoshi

Work is always good for the
body and restful for the mind.

The body remembers past pleasures
and on being made aware of them,
floods the mind with sweetness.

Cyril Connolly

**Be good to your heart if you want it
to be good to you.**

Eat as much as you need but
never as much as you can.

**Your body will age. But that is no
excuse for you to get older.**

Keep calm for your stomach's sake. An unquiet mind wrecks the digestion.

Your body can always do more than you think when a determined spirit drives it.

Have you ever seen these ads showing before and after plastic surgery pictures? Isn't it odd how the people always looked so much better *before*?

Make sure that you always have good reason to hold your head high.

The body is an instrument that only gives off music when it is used as a body. Always an orchestra, and just as music traverses walls, so sensuality traverses the body and reaches up to ecstasy.

Anaïs Nin

Think with your whole body.
Taisen Deshimaru

If you feel uncomfortable but don't know why, don't ignore it. Your body never sends pointless messages.

Don't think of doctors as people to go to when you're sick. Think of them as people who can help you avoid getting sick.

Love will warm you better than the warmest coat.

Say only as much as you need and people will listen to you. If you chatter like a monkey you'll be ignored.

Don't take yourself too seriously. People who can laugh at themselves make the best friends.

**If you smile you'll make friends.
Scowl and you'll get wrinkles.**

We should consider every day
lost on which we have not
danced at least once.

Friedrich Nietzsche

Our own physical body possesses a wisdom which we who inhabit the body lack. We give it orders which make no sense.

Henry Miller

Love at first sight really exists. Our eyes are often wiser than we are.

People who are uncertain in their hearts are the most dogmatic in their minds.

Act happy, think happy, and the odds are that you will be happy.

People cannot read your kind thoughts. You must show them by your actions that you love them.

Language, which does not acknowledge the body, cannot acknowledge life.

John Lahr

Be energetic and full of enthusiasm and your body will repay your efforts many times over.

You are all that you will ever have in this world. It makes sense to take good care of such a prized possession.

Be flexible. The soft and supple are the companions of life. The hard and rigid are the companions of death.

Don't let yourself speak harshly to others. Hard words harm both the speaker and the listener.

In your speech, you should be simple, natural, and unaffected. To be that natural doesn't come naturally, it takes practice.

Do not worry that your body has a limited life. Think how much worse off you'd be if it didn't.

It is a shame that bodies that can be so good at loving are so often used for fighting.

Be ready to embrace change. It is the very soul of life and should not be resisted.

Change your ideas like you change your clothes—and for much the same reason; old ideas that have not been rethought for a while can begin to stink.

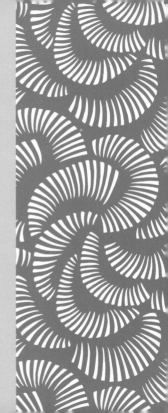

You are never too old to learn a new skill. Why not please your body by teaching it some new tricks?

Getting older isn't a problem. It is the thought of aging that is the problem.

A good long walk in the countryside followed by a hot cup of coffee when you get home. What could be a greater success than that?

The human body is vapor materialized by sunshine mixed with the life of the stars.

Paracelsus

Some people are careless of physical danger and seem like heroes. But the real heroism comes from thinking bravely.

When angry never say the first thing that comes into your head. Breathe deeply, calm down, and say something wiser.

Far from distrusting the temporal delights that come through the body, we should abandon ourselves to them with confidence. The way of the sense is the way of life. It is the people with their hands in the till and their eyes on heaven who ruin existence…. Without doubt half the ethical rules they din into our ears are designed to keep you at work.

Llewelyn Powys

We do not have unlimited energy or unlimited time. Make sure you spend yours on things that matter.

Never kill the fly on your friend's head
with a hatchet.

Chinese proverb

**We always push harder
against opposition.**

It is surprising how many people, when
digging themselves a hole, find it simply
impossible to stop.

**It is our great fortune that the body
has no memory of pain. If it did,
would mothers go through giving
birth more than once?**

The body needs more than food, clothing, and shelter. It also needs work.

Travel widely in body and in mind. We need constant new experience to help us grow.

A man's height gives him a different outlook on his environment and so changes his character.

W. Somerset Maugham

Activity is fine, but never mistake it for achievement.

Without the body, the wisdom of the larger self cannot be known.

John Conger

If you can honestly say, "Wherever I lay my head is my home," you have a great freedom.

The mouth has many uses and of all those, giving advice to others is probably the least useful. Keep your mouth shut until advice is asked for and even then, be careful how you give it.

Feelings are there to be expressed, and our bodies are perfectly adapted for doing that. Never make a virtue of keeping your feelings to yourself.

If you want a thing done, go; if not, send.

Benjamin Franklin

Comfort of your body will only work if your mind is at peace.

Life is not a matter of aging but of becoming.

You can wear nothing half as becoming to you as a smile.

The word arse is as much god as the word face. It must be so; otherwise, you cut off your god at the waist.

D. H. Lawrence

Always act your shoe size, not your age.

From the middle of life onward, only he remains vitally alive who is ready to die with life.

Carl Jung

If we work at it only the body ages and within we stay as young as ever.

If you sit around long enough age will catch up with you. Get up and run around and it might miss you.

Old bodies can still
be inhabited by
young, lively minds.

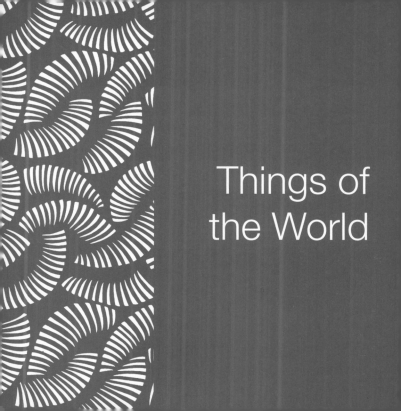

Things of
the World

Work at being
indispensable
and you will
succeed.
Act as though
you are
indispensable
and you
will fail.

Carry your achievements lightly and you will achieve more.

The more you attempt the more you will succeed in doing.

It's hard to tell which gets knocked the most, the success or the failure, but it's mighty close.

Kin Hubbard

It takes far more strength to conquer parts of yourself than it does to conquer the whole world.

Do not confuse success with income. Making money for its own sake is a sad and empty activity.

To fail is always sad but to give up without trying is far worse.

Everyone is a potential winner. Those who push hard enough for long enough are the ones who make it.

If you want to succeed in life, the first step is to do your very best with whatever job you have in hand right now.

The one way to succeed is to determine that you will be the very best person you are capable of being.

If you can actually count your money, then you're not a rich man.
J. Paul Getty

The world is crying out for you to say, "Yes!"

Spiderwebs united can bind a lion.
African proverb

Don't dissipate your energy on a hundred different things. Find what is worth doing and do it with all your strength.

The real pleasure of success lies in your ability to share it.

Success that is gained by clambering over the bodies of failures is a terrible thing.

The goal all of us must aim to achieve is simply leaving the world a better place than when we came into it.

Getting even distracts from getting ahead.

If you never fail then you're clearly not trying hard enough.

In a gentle way you can shake the world.

Mahatma Gandhi

To succeed you must be utterly truthful with yourself about your motives.

You only find that which you bring with you.

All success in this world comes down to hard work.

It is no use walking anywhere to preach unless our walking is our preaching.

St. Francis of Assisi

It is the quality, not the quantity, of what you do that determines your success.

Change is the key to life.
If you work in accord with
change you will succeed;
if you resist you will fail.

**Life is like this: You can complain
that blackberries have thorns or you
can be happy that thorny brambles
bear delicious blackberries.**

You usually know what you should do. Success comes from having the determination and courage to do it.

A tree that can fill the span of a man's arms grows from a downy tip; a terrace nine stories high rises from hodfuls of earth; a journey of a thousand miles starts from beneath one's feet.

Tao Te Ching

Simplify. Nothing truly great is ever complicated.

The world is full of unlimited wealth but all you get to do is borrow some of it for a while.

To whom much is given, much is required.

John F. Kennedy

Many great men climb to prominence on the corpses of their fellow men. Is attaining wealth worth all this?

Keep your feet firmly on the ground but let your thoughts rise to the heavens.

Remember that it is not all about you.

Human life is a story of continual but slow progress. We each get to add our own piece, be it great or small.

The rich are not necessarily those with money.

Eighty percent of success is showing up.

Woody Allen

Never take your eye off the ball.

You can only succeed at things to
which you give your heart.

**Success comes at a price.
Before you seek it make
sure you can afford to pay.**

The only person who
knows whether you are
a success is you.

We've all heard about the celebrity who works all his life to be well known and then has to wear sunglasses to keep himself from being recognized. Did he succeed?

Serving others is always a powerful kind of success.

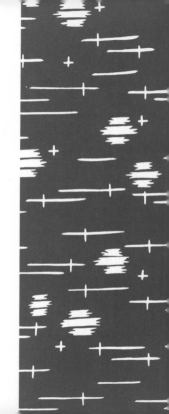

No one wants to know about the storms you met, the rocks you avoided, or the sharks that failed to eat you. All they want to know is whether you got the ship home in one piece.

A man digs a hole. As the hole gets deeper so does his investment in it. Soon it becomes *his* hole in which he has invested time and energy. Before you start digging, make sure you are in the right place!

Fear of failure is failure.

You don't get the best fruit unless you are willing to climb to the top of the tree.

What do you want others to say of you? Now you know what it will take to succeed.

There are always problems, but they are like rungs on a ladder; the more we solve the higher we climb.

It is one thing to climb the ladder of success but it takes talent to be sure that you have the ladder leaning against the right wall.

When you come to the end of your rope...tie a knot and hang on.

Franklin D. Roosevelt

Life flows with you
if only you will let it.

Just because you cannot achieve everything you wish, that is no reason to attempt nothing.

No one is born a success. It is something that you have to get for yourself.

The greatest spur to success is the praise of others.

Success is 90 percent enthusiasm.

Neither a lofty degree of intelligence nor imagination nor both together go to the making of genius. Love, love, love, that is the soul of genius.

Wolfgang Amadeus Mozart

Acquiring things may well give you the appearance of success but the reality will still evade you.

No matter how many people applaud you, you will only have succeeded if you can applaud yourself.

There is always a way to climb any mountain.

The greatest success is when you finally learn who you are and have the courage to be that person.

Someone with belief in his heart and fire in his belly is worth a hundred who are only doing a job.

According to science, the bumblebee should never get off the ground. It must be his strong belief that gets him airborne.

Getting what you need in life is more important than getting what you want.

You'll never succeed on your own. Be grateful to those whose efforts help you on your way.

Success is like rock climbing—it's best not to look down!

Never let success make you arrogant. That merely cheapens your achievement.

Let your achievements speak for themselves. Blowing your own trumpet decreases the respect others have for you.

As long as you think of work as work only, you will never really succeed. You must love what you do with a great passion before you can really achieve all that you want.

Every individual has a place to fill in the world and is important, in some respect, whether he chooses to be so or not.

Nathaniel Hawthorne

People are fickle—no sooner have they built you up than they want to tear you down.

Small triumphs are triumphs nonetheless. You do not have to be Alexander the Great in order to be a success.

Don't waste time. If you want to succeed you must make every day count.

Doing a little every day without fail is better than wild enthusiasm that peters out before you reach your goal.

Success depends on taking good advice, especially your own.

No one can guarantee success in war, but only deserve it.

Winston Churchill

Good ideas are a dime a dozen. It is the ability to make them work that distinguishes the able from the average.

Be nice to people as you journey through life. You never know when you may meet them again.

Count on success but always plan for failure.

You should be like a good fire and consume yourself utterly in everything that you do.

If you listen to others all you will hear are endless reasons why what you are doing won't work. Listen instead to the prompting of your own heart.

The fact that the leaders of all the great religions were poor men who lived simply should tell us a lot about how to lead our lives.

What would you want to see written on your tombstone? That gives you some idea of what success means to you.

Success is not when people want your autograph—that's fame and goes as quickly as it came. Success is like a monument that survives long after you are gone.

The best soldier does not attack.
The superior fighter succeeds
without violence. The greatest
conqueror wins without struggle.
The most successful manager
leads without dictating. This is
intelligent non-aggressiveness.
This is called the mastery of men.

Tao Te Ching

Getting what you get is
good, but wanting what
you get is an art.

There is no point in achieving success if it leaves you no room for living.

Remember this: no one on his deathbed ever wishes he'd spent more time at work.

When you succeed, you may well find that the part you really enjoyed was the struggle you had along the way.

The manner in which you get what you want governs what sort of person you'll have become by the time your objective is achieved.

To be arrogant and hard-hearted when fortune has smiled on you is to invite misfortune.

Think to yourself, "If I put all my effort into this, who will be the happier for it?"

**Our lives all come to the same
end eventually. Mind that what
you do was worth the time you
spent on it.**

To succeed you need a
dream. It is the spark of
inspiration that makes
the perspiration worthwhile.

A good plan violently executed right now is far better than a perfect plan executed next week.

General George Patton

Before you succeed people will be anxious to tell you how wrong you are. Of course, after you've succeeded they will tell you how they had every faith in you right from the beginning.

The pack moves at the speed of the leader.

To advance you need to use the past as a springboard not a hammock.

Nothing ever suppresses a truly creative mind.

One of the greatest pleasures of life is to succeed where everyone said success was impossible.

People who say "It may not work" or "What are we going to do if it fails?" do not have the credentials to be businessmen. If there is only a one percent chance of success, a true businessperson sees that one percent as the spark to light a fire.

Kim Woo Choong

Let your effort be like water eroding rock. Don't struggle foolishly but never give up trying.

To be defeated in a great and noble struggle is not a failure.

Pick your battles carefully. No general wins every fight.

Each of us is capable of improving the world in some way. Most of us will make only a small difference but it is still important that we make it.

Expert advice is valuable. Experts know exactly what is impossible and, what's more, why it is impossible. All you then have to do is prove them wrong.

It is important to take chances. That is what makes the best of life.

When you work for money, remember that you are selling chunks of your life. Make sure that you value what you get in return.

You can't change where the wind blows but you can adjust your sails so that you use it most advantageously.

What's money? A man is a success if he gets up in the morning and goes to bed at night and in between does what he wants to do.

To succeed you must be where the buck stops.

We can all think beautiful thoughts. But the ability to translate them into action and the action into results are the measures of success.

Give the world the very best that you have and the world will return the favor.

Creativity can solve any problem. It is a question of letting your originality take charge.

Always be a lot smarter than you look. It gives you a hidden advantage.

Don't let the things you can't do get in the way of those you can do.

Everything was difficult until you found out how easy it really was.

The world admires the successful but not as much as it loves the kind-hearted.

Do not make a god of success. It will never repay all the devotion you give to it.

It may be corny to say that the best things in life are free, but it is also true.

Work for the love of the work and not for the love of the rewards.

The greatest success is to put your heart and soul into all you do.

Your reputation follows you wherever you go and lives on after you die. Never buy success at the expense of reputation.

Life is short. Never be so busy that you forget to live to the full.

Opportunities
multiply as they
are seized.

Colin Wilson

Those
We Love

Every day we all give something of ourselves to those around us. It is up to us to ensure that we give the best that we can.

Families are the bricks we use to build civilization.

Nothing is harder to
do than raise a family.
Nothing is so worthwhile.

**Not all families are happy, but
happy or not, we are tied to a family
for life. Better make the best of it.**

Perhaps the greatest social service
that can be rendered by anybody
to this country and to mankind is to
bring up a family.

George Bernard Shaw

Raising kids successfully
isn't rocket science—it's
much harder than that!

**Loving people is about accepting
them as they are and not trying to
change them into what we want
them to be.**

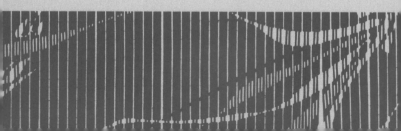

The most important thing a father can do for his children is to love their mother.

Theodore Hesburgh

People want passion and will go to any lengths to get it. Sadly, passion is fleeting and only true friendship lasts a lifetime.

To marry
one who
becomes
your closest
friend is
good fortune
beyond value.

A family is the safety
net that gives you the
confidence to climb high.

**We only succeed as humans when
we give ourselves unconditionally
to those closest to us.**

What your family
wants most from
you is you.

Raising children requires no license, no training, and no experience. They don't even come with a book of instructions. It is a wonder that so many people make such a good job of it.

People talk about the "nuclear family." Is that because of all the warmth it supplies?

Family members frequently drive one another crazy. But who else knows so much about you and still manages to love you?

The family, that dear octopus from whose tentacles we never quite escape, nor in our innermost hearts never quite wish to.

Dodie Smith

Love is immune to success or failure. It just happens and there is absolutely nothing you can do about it.

A large part of success as a parent lies in being there when your kids need something to kick, secure in the knowledge that it won't kick back too hard.

Most success is fleeting but a good relationship keeps getting better.

Relationships are
like automobiles:
to last they need
regular attention.

**Habit is the great enemy
of love.**

Love is never an overnight
success. It grows slowly
and becomes sturdy like
a great and stately tree.

You're a success when there are people who worry about you.

You'll never amount to much unless you let your children teach you how.

The best relationships are based on communication. You don't have to say anything profound but make sure you always keep talking.

Choose friends with care. The good ones are made to last a long time.

Who would miss you if you weren't here? You need to be important to the people around you or you're not important at all.

Where there are friends there is wealth.

Titus Muccius Plautus

Nor need we power or splendor,
wide hall or lordly dome;
The good, the true, the tender—
these form the wealth of home.

Sarah J. Hale

Winning is always good but winning friends is the best.

People will turn to you if you are interested in them. It's not so easy if you expect them to be interested in you.

Success is only worth having when you have people to share it with.

Don't pour your love over someone like maple syrup. Too much sweetness is always a bad idea.

A hundred men can make an encampment but it takes a woman to make a home.

Chinese proverb

You can search the whole world for the things you think you need. Only when you return home do you get what you really need.

The best you can do for your children is to have an unshakable belief in them.

We are stronger together than we are on our own. When you are united with someone you love, there is nothing you cannot do.

Relationships that are based on blood are not complete. They must be based on love and respect as well.

However many people admire and respect you be sure that your family knows the truth.

People are governed by emotion much more than logic. A warm heart will win more friends than a cool head.

If you really want the truth, you will often get an uncomfortable amount of it from children.

Never patronize children;
keep in mind the adults
they will soon become.

When you love people, serving them is a pleasure and not a duty.

Doing things for your children is a pleasure but teaching them to do things for themselves is an achievement.

Most people do better when they strive to succeed, not for themselves but for those they love.

Families are never easy, and sometimes we think they are impossible. But in the end, and against all the odds, mutual love pulls everyone through.

**People are never compatible
at the beginning of a marriage.
It's whether you become
compatible that matters.**

We love our children and treat them
much like cuddly toys. The test is
whether we can still love them when
they are clearly intent on becoming
people in their own right.

The key to a successful relationship is in learning to be the sort of person you would like to be with.

A relationship is only any good if you think more about what you put into it than what you're getting out of it.

Almost all the good things we do
are done to please our loved ones.
The bad things are usually those
we do to please ourselves.

**If you don't value the opinions
of your children, you are doing
both them and yourself a
great disservice.**

To be loved by others you
need to believe yourself to
be lovable.

Respect is the cornerstone of any relationship. Once that goes out the window, love is lost.

Having children makes you no more a parent than having a piano makes you a pianist.

Michael Levine

Old friends are the best. They will never let you get away from the person you really are.

A good marriage is never too serene. If you can't argue, shout, laugh, and cry then your partnership is lacking something vital.

Push each other to be the best you are capable of being. Partners have a unique power to bring out the best in each other.

To love and be loved, what in the world is greater than that?

Fights aren't bad. They clear the air and stop you from harboring resentment. But observe one rule: no one goes to bed mad.

If love is a one-way street it can never last. The traffic must flow constantly in both directions.

That is why marriage is so much more interesting than divorce, because it is the only known example of the happy meeting of the immovable object and the irresistible force. So I hope husbands and wives will continue to debate and combat over everything debatable and combatable. Because I believe a little incompatibility is the spice of life.

Ogden Nash

All relationships are about sharing. It doesn't matter too much what you share, because the act of sharing in itself binds us together.

In families it pays to listen. It may be difficult with all the shouting that goes on but it is more important to listen than to talk.

Learn to understand what your family members are telling you when they say nothing. Many important messages are conveyed by silence.

Never be afraid to be vulnerable in front of those you love. They'll love you even more for showing a little human weakness.

Criticizing those we love is always tough on both parties but, if it is done with love, then it is done for the best.

Never lose sight of what
you want your children
to remember about you
when they are grown up.

**No matter how long you've been
together never get out of the habit
of expressing affection.**

If a friend does you a favor
remember to return it.

No success in public life can compensate for failure in the home.

Benjamin Disraeli

When you decide on a partner for life don't analyze the choice but go with your hunch. Your inner voice knows things that your head doesn't understand.

When you're annoyed with one of your family members say so; don't let resentment fester within you.

Don't worry if you don't get along with your teenagers. No one does. They are on a journey and will be back soon.

Giving advice is always tempting but useless. Family members don't want your advice unless they ask for it—and often not even then.

Never praise another woman to your wife—and especially never praise her cooking!

Your children should feel safe, wanted, and loved. They won't necessarily admit to any of this.

When kids get to the, "I'm grown-up and don't need you anymore" stage, be sure that they aren't and they do.

The only successful way to teach children the important lessons of life is by example.

Children will detect the truth about the relationship of their parents no matter what is done to hide it.

A family is never a democracy.

Encourage your children all the time. It is not enough to let them guess that you approve.

A wife is often the chief architect of her husband's character.

Don't live your life through your children. It is not their job to fulfill your own unfulfilled dreams.

Eat together. It is a wonderful and civilized tradition that we are in danger of losing.

One word frees us of all the weight and pain of life; that word is love.

Sophocles

Don't be afraid to do things differently from your parents. They teach us by their mistakes as well as their successes.

Any boy can get a
girl. To keep one
takes a man.

A family is a team effort and, like any team, it works best when everyone pulls together.

Your children might do many things that would make you disappointed or angry but it is unlikely that they could do anything that would make you stop loving them.

Many a man who could make a hundred employees shake in their shoes will be very careful to take his own shoes off when he comes home from the office.

Families invented the art of the compromise solution.

Always remember that two monologues never make a dialogue.

Never be afraid to be silly. Your family is the one place you can get away with it.

**Too many parents make life hard
for their children by trying, too
zealously, to make it easy for them.**
Johann Wolfgang von Goethe

Pleasure usually takes
the form of me and now;
joy is us and always.

Marvin J. Ashton

Never say the unkind thing that immediately comes to mind. Pause, and say something warm and generous.

To the world you are one person, but if you're lucky, to one person you are the world.

Love is about who you want to be with and who you couldn't bear to be without.

You need a lot of forgiveness in a relationship. Only the strong are truly able to forgive.

Being prepared to admit you were wrong is like a great supporting beam in the edifice of marriage.

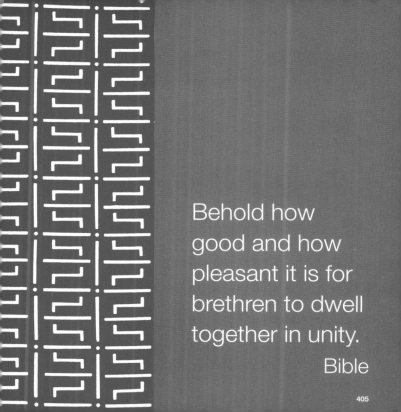

Behold how
good and how
pleasant it is for
brethren to dwell
together in unity.

Bible

Love happens to a man
and a woman who don't
know each other yet.

**You think that you help your
children to grow up. In fact, it
is mostly the other way around.**

If you have a good marriage and
a happy family don't let this make
you smug. Try spreading some of
that happiness around.

You can't be successfully married to another unless you are divorced from yourself.

A good marriage
halves your grief
and doubles your joy.

**Smile at each other, smile at your
wife, smile at your husband, smile
at your children, smile at each
other—it doesn't matter who it is—
and that will help you to grow up in
greater love for each other.**

Mother Teresa

**Love is the only sane
and satisfactory answer
to the problem of
human existence.**

Erich Fromm

Partners continue to
love each other in
spite of all their faults.

The difference between a successful marriage and an unsuccessful one is the number of things that are left unsaid.

For me, the highest level of sexual excitement is in a monogamous relationship.

Warren Beatty

What keeps people together for 30 or 40 years is not passion but a kind and gentle companionship.

The secret of a
happy marriage
is still secret.

A man without a wife is like a
vase without flowers.

African proverb

**There is no substitute for the
comfort supplied by the utterly
taken-for-granted relationship.**

Iris Murdoch

Love teaches even asses
to dance.

French proverb

Friendship may eventually turn to love, but not the other way around.

Don't judge those you would love.

A king, realizing his incompetence, can either delegate or abdicate his duties. A father can do neither.

Marlene Dietrich

Age does not protect you from love but love to some extent protects you from age.

If you love someone set them free. If they come back then you know that it was love.

414

You will never lose anything by loving but you will always lose by holding back.

Moderation in all things— except love.

Love is not about
finding the perfect
person but about
two people sharing
their imperfections.

The
Creative
Urge

Being creative is the nearest
we get to playing God.

Creativity comes from the huge part of
the mind that is invisible. It goes against
the grain to trust in what you can't see
but, unless you learn to do it, you will
not create anything worth a damn.

**To be a creative person you
must encourage the flow of ideas.
Most of them won't work but you
will conquer eventually by sheer
force of numbers.**

To be creative successfully you must toss out the maps and try to forge new paths through uncharted territory.

Anyone at all can have a bright idea, but the creative person is the one with the energy and skill to polish an idea until it gleams.

You can force people into manual labor but you cannot make them create. They cannot even make themselves do it. You have to understand how to let it happen spontaneously.

Being creative is like fishing in the ocean: You're not quite sure what's down there but if you stick with it long enough you'll catch something.

A hunch is your creativity tapping you on the shoulder trying to get a word in edgewise.

To be creative is to empty yourself of habitual thought and allow ideas to flow into you from God knows where.

People wait for inspiration but that's no good. It is when you have tried and tried to no avail that inspiration is most likely to strike.

If you sincerely believe that you are a well of ideas and that no matter how many times you dip into the well it will still be full, then it is very likely to be true.

You never know what sort of bright ideas are going to come. Often you don't get the one you need at the moment you need it, but if you're smart you'll keep all of them on the principle that they will come in useful one day. You will never be disappointed.

Creation is a
drug I can't
do without.
Cecil B. DeMille

**Creativity is not
necessarily
about finding
something new
but about
finding a new
way to look at
what is familiar.**

Thoughts create a new heaven, a new firmament, a new source of energy, from which new arts flow. When a man undertakes to create something, he establishes a new heaven.

Philippus A. Paracelsus

In order to be creative you need great courage.

People will only admire creativity once it is has been made safe. While it is actually happening, they will hide as though it was an unexploded bomb.

If you want to succeed creatively you must never ask, "How did we do this the last time?"

All creativity arises
from enthusiasm.

We are the most inquisitive species ever to walk the Earth. The secret of our creativity is simply that we cannot resist asking, "Why?"

The deadliest enemy of
creativity is common sense.

It is hard to be creative and not to believe in God.

Leisure and creativity almost never go hand in hand. To be creative a certain pressure is necessary.

You are creative the moment your native stupidity drops away and you say, "Of course!"

To be creative you need
the sort of mind that
enjoys a good mystery.

The things we fear most in
organizations—fluctuations,
disturbances, imbalances—are
the primary sources of creativity.

Margaret J. Wheatley

It took Mr. Biro
a few minutes
to come up
with the idea
of a ballpoint
pen and many
years of
intense effort
to learn how to
make it work.

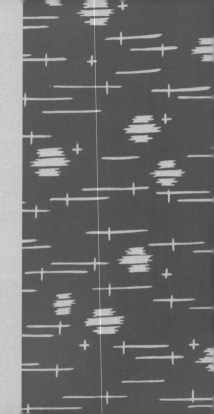

Creativity has become very popular largely because it is mysteriously linked to our libido.

Chaos is the great ally of the creative mind. The more you mix things up, the better your chances of finding interesting connections.

A good idea will seem obvious the moment someone else has thought of it.

Education is much to blame for stifling creativity. Once you teach children the right way to do everything you preclude them from finding interesting new wrong ways.

Creativity is allowing yourself to make mistakes. Art is knowing which ones to keep.

Scott Adams

There is no end to creativity, nor does it have any aim. It is a constant dripping of that sweet creative juice into a receptive mind.

Failure should never discourage you from being creative. Some of the most important notions have sprung from projects that, at first sight, appeared to have failed.

Intelligence and creativity are not linked. Some of the dullest people are enormously clever.

Creativity is available to us in all areas of our lives. Whether you want to paint a picture, solve a problem, or simply fix a hole in the roof there is always one beautiful new way in which to do it.

The urge to destroy is a creative urge.

Mikhail Bakunin

**Everyone can try to be creative
and some will succeed better than
others will. In people of genius the
creativity rages like a forest fire.**

Many authors experience the
feeling that someone else writes
their books through them.

**To see is to forget the name of
the thing one sees.**

Paul Valery

The creative urge is as insistent and uncomfortable as the urge to scratch an itchy nose.

The creative person is reborn every day.

A good teacher is the one who can awaken in pupils not the thirst for knowledge but the joy of creation.

Life is ungraspable—far beyond our capacity to understand. Yet it is this very elusive quality that urges us to seek understanding and makes us creative people.

Don't think. Thinking is the enemy of creativity. It's self-conscious, and anything self-conscious is lousy. You can't try to do things. You simply must do things.

Ray Bradbury

Children are naturally and spontaneously creative. Sadly, many adults see it as their duty to cure them and teach them the proper way to act.

Life is all about creative problem solving. A lack of problems would be a kind of death.

People have evolved by a mixture of competition and cooperation. But in the end, it is the creative, cooperative spirit that wins the day.

Your creativity is like a lamp that can illuminate even the darkest corners of your existence. All you have to do is shine it in the desired direction.

Don't let anyone interfere with your creativity. You might just as well let him or her shut off your air supply.

Every author knows that there are no new stories but there are hundreds of ways to tell an old story that make it seem new.

If everyone understands what you've done then you haven't been creative enough. If someone says, "Oh, I'm not sure you should have done it like that," you're on the right track.

Once you have stretched your mind to encompass a new idea it will never shrink back to the way it was before.

Nothing is more difficult to achieve than simplicity.

Never be afraid to ask the stupid question. Such questions have often turned out to be the very spark needed for a creative leap forward.

Do not impose your ideas and opinions on children. Your job is to encourage them to find their own.

Never take this life for granted. Once it no longer seems like a miracle you are lost.

There is no happiness like that of creativity. It fires the soul in a way that mere money or material possessions never could.

Life is a process of constant discovery. If it weren't so, we'd never bother getting out of bed.

The true wealth of the modern world lies in its ideas.

Some people worry about the speed of our progress. They find the constant flood of new ideas threatening. On the contrary, it is the most hopeful sign that people are not just clever apes but are beings capable of climbing relentlessly toward a distant goal.

The speed of recent human progress is truly miraculous. Just think: There are people still alive who remember a time before powered flight.

True art is characterized by an irresistible urge in the creative artist.

Albert Einstein

Everything that makes the world a more pleasant place to live is the fruit of someone's original thinking.

When I think of all the crap I learned in high school, it's a wonder I can think at all.

Paul Simon

Our thought is limitless. It can take us to unknown worlds, indeed right to the ends of the universe.

The creative person wants to be a know-it-all. He wants to know about all kinds of things: ancient history, nineteenth-century mathematics, current manufacturing techniques, flower arranging, and hog futures. Because he never knows when these ideas might come together to form a new idea. It may happen six minutes later or six months, or six years down the road. But he has faith that it will happen.

Carl Ally

To solve a problem you must sneak up on it from an unusual direction.

Believe in life. We come out of nothing and return to nothing, yet what we think of as "nothing" seems extraordinarily productive.

If you truly care about what you do, then you'll find a way to do it creatively. Habit is reserved for those things we don't give a damn about.

Tranquillity has its place and can be great for recharging our batteries. But in the end we are creatures that thrive on activity.

Don't write long letters. It takes trouble and talent to express yourself succinctly.

Inspiration is a wonderful thing but once you have a bright idea it has to be honed, sometimes for years, before it is sharp enough to cut a new path.

Being creative in the service of mere efficiency is bad. The creative impulse should be allowed to flourish for its own sake. It is only then that it produces revolutionary ideas.

You can make a whole career out of an idea, as long as it is a really good one.

Politics is the art of the possible; creativity is the art of the impossible.

Ben Okri

What we have created in life is the legacy we leave to the world.

Think the unthinkable.

Never be satisfied. Put aside whatever you have created and try again. Improvements always can be made.

Originality is this: go as far as you possibly can—then take one more step.

If you don't encourage your creative spark, you'll find yourself becoming listless and dull. You don't have to be Shakespeare but you should give your brains a good workout for the sake of your mind.

If an idea is complicated assume that you've got it wrong. All good ideas are stunningly simple.

On the border between sleep and wakefulness is a place where, if we are quick, we can capture ideas that float near the surface of the unconscious. It is not easy to fish these waters but the catch is often worth the trouble.

Go outside and mow the lawn. It's amazing how many good ideas will emerge if you distract yourself by doing something mundane.

Creativity is a little like being struck by lightning. You can't make it happen but you can put yourself in a position where it might.

Never think for a moment that you are not clever enough to be creative. Brains have little to do with it. What you need is to be able to open that channel between your conscious mind and the great ocean of the unconscious—an ability possessed by the most surprising people. The only way you will know whether you are one of them is to try.

It is not your place to decide whether your creativity is good or not. You do what you can do as well as you know how to do it. Others may well recognize genius that you didn't know you possessed.

Always think to yourself, "My best work is still to come."

The best thing in life is not to find answers to questions but to discover answers that provoke new questions.

If you want your creativity to flourish you must foster a sense of wonder in yourself. If you allow yourself to think of life as boring and predictable creative thought becomes impossible.

Bright ideas are as slippery as fish. Once you have one make sure you write it down before it gets away!

When the bright ideas refuse to flow it is a mistake to panic. Anxiety is always the enemy of creative thought. Relax, think of something else, and wait patiently for the flow to resume.

Bright ideas are the oil that keeps your brain turning over smoothly.

Let your mind go where it will. Do not try to beat it into submission and make it do what you want. Your mind is much wiser than you are and will show you interesting paths if you let it.

The creation of something new is not accomplished by the intellect but by the play instinct acting from inner necessity. The creative mind plays with the objects it loves.

Carl Gustav Jung

Competing with other creative people is a waste of your time and impairs your ability. Concentrate on maintaining your own creative spirit and let others do what they will.

You must always have faith in your own ability. There are plenty of other people who will happily tell you what you're doing wrong.

There are no impossible problems, only ones for which you have not yet found the solution.

Your life will reflect your state of mind. A creative person is in for an exciting time.

Some people have the ability to inspire you. Always look out for such people and make them your friends.

Creativity represents a miraculous coming together of the uninhibited energy of the child with its apparent opposite and enemy— the sense of order imposed on the disciplined adult intelligence.

Norman Podhoretz

Dream the impossible and you'll find ways to make it possible.

To reach for the stars—even if you don't get there—is better than never having tried.

Your creativity is a flame within you. For it to burn bright you must keep it fueled with hope.

Creativity is contagious. Don't be surprised if your efforts inspire the work of others.

Don't measure yourself by what you have accomplished but by what you can accomplish.

The prospect of success in achieving our most cherished dream is not without its terrors. Who is more deprived and alone than the man who has achieved his dream?

Brendan Francis

What you see depends on what you look for. If you look for a world of miracles you will certainly find them.

It is better to fail in originality than to succeed in imitation.

Herman Melville

When you reach a goal pat yourself on the back, then forget about it and set off in search of the next one.

The best thing about creativity is the way you manage to think of things you are sure you could never have thought of.

The advantage of an untidy mind is that you are always stumbling over things and saying, "That's exactly what I wanted."

When I am working on a problem
I never think about beauty. I only
think about how to solve the problem.
But when I have finished, if the solution
is not beautiful, I know it is wrong.

Buckminster Fuller

Let go of the known, the safe, and the predictable. Open yourself to that which is most unexpected.

As with seeds falling on stony ground you'll find that not all your ideas germinate. Don't let that discourage you—keep producing more ideas.

Average people think that an unusual idea is too crazy to work. It takes exceptional people to think, "That's an interesting idea. How can I make it work?"

The writer who possesses the creative gift owns something of which he is not always master— something that at times strangely wills and works for itself.

Charlotte Brontë

There is nothing as powerful as an idea that is having its day.

Always look for that which is odd and out of the way. It is there that you will find inspiration waiting.

This "telephone" has too many shortcomings to be seriously considered as a means of communication. The device is inherently of no value to us.

Western Union internal memo, 1876

Man's reach should exceed his grasp, or what's a heaven for?

Robert Browning

No idea is ever wasted. An idea that doesn't work should be put to one side and saved for the day when it throws light upon another possibility.

Creativity is hard. But the alternative is much harder and less fun.

Creativity is constantly looking for relationships where common sense tells us none exist.

Don't always go with the flow.
Only dead fish swim with the stream.

Come to the edge. We might fall.
Come to the edge. It's too high!
Come to the edge! And they came,
and he pushed…and they flew.

Christopher Logue

Published by MQ Publications Limited
12 The Ivories
6–8 Northampton Street
London, N1 2HY
email: mail@mqpublications.com
website: www.mqpublications.com

Design: Philippa Jarvis

ISBN: 1-84072-730-6

10 9 8 7 6 5 4 3 2 1

Printed and bound in China